Travel Guide To

Corfu, GREECE

From Sunsets to Cuisine: Must-See Spots Revealed!

Wybikes Hinton

COPYRIGHT NOTICE

This publication is copyright protected. This is only for personal use. No part of this publication may be, including but not limited to, reproduced, in any form or medium, stored in a data retrieval system or transmitted by or through any means, without prior written permission from the Author / Publisher.

Legal action will be pursued if this is breached.

DISCLAIMER

Please note that the information contained within this document is for educational purposes only. The information contained herein has been obtained from sources believed to be reliable at the time of publication. The opinions expressed herein are subject to change without notice.

Readers acknowledge that the Author / Publisher is not engaging in rendering legal, financial or professional advice. The Publisher / Author disclaims all warranties as to the accuracy, completeness, or adequacy of such information.

The Publisher assumes no liability for errors, omissions, or inadequacies in the information contained herein or from the interpretations thereof. The publisher / Author specifically disclaims any liability from the use or application of the information contained herein or from the interpretations thereof.

TABLE OF CONTENT

Copyright Notice
Disclaimer
Table of Content
Introduction
Welcome To Corfu, Greece!

Welcome to Corfu

Brief Overview of Corfu

Why Visit Corfu?

Tips for Visitors

About This Guide

How to Use This Guide

Chapter 1
Getting to Know Corfu

Corfu: An Island Overview

Geography and Climate of Corfu

Corfu's History and Culture

Language and Communication

Navigating the Island

Chapter 2
Planning Your Trip to Corfu

Best Time to Visit Corfu

How to Get to Corfu

Transportation on the Island

Where to Stay in Corfu

Choosing Your Accommodation

Accessibility and Special Needs

Chapter 3
Accommodation Options in Corfu

Overview of Accommodation Options

Luxury Resorts

Budget-Friendly Hotels

Boutique Guesthouses

Unique Stays

Top Recommended Hotels and Resorts

Choosing the Right Accommodation for You

Booking Tips and Tricks

Chapter 4
Exploring Corfu Town

Corfu Town: A Cultural Hub

Corfu Port and Waterfront

Museums and Historical Sites

Local Markets and Shopping

Dining and Cuisine in Corfu Town

Nightlife and Entertainment Options

Conclusion

Chapter 5
Top Tourist Attractions in Corfu

Achilleion Palace

Old Fortress of Corfu

Liston Promenade

Paleokastritsa Monastery

Sidari Beach and Canal d'Amour

Chapter 6
Outdoor Activities in Corfu

Hiking and Nature Trails

Watersports and Beach Activities

Cycling and Biking Routes

Boat Tours and Excursions

Fishing and Snorkeling Spots

Chapter 7
Cultural Experiences in Corfu

Traditional Greek Festivals and Events

Local Arts and Crafts Workshops

Cooking Classes and Culinary Tours

Music and Dance Performances

Religious Observances and Pilgrimages

Cultural Heritage Conservation Endeavors

Chapter 8
Dining and Cuisine in Corfu

Authentic Greek Tavernas and Eateries

Corfu's Seafood Delights

Local Delights and Desserts

Olive Oil Tasting and Production

Wine and Ouzo Tastings

Recommended Dining Experiences

Chapter 9
Shopping and Markets in Corfu

Souvenir Shops and Gift Boutiques

Local Crafts and Artisanal Offerings

Fresh Produce Markets and Stalls

Traditional Greek Products

Bargaining Tips and Tactics

Food and Wine Souvenirs Shopping

Chapter 10
Day Trips and Excursions from Corfu

Paxos and Antipaxos Islands

Albania: Saranda and Butrint

Parga and Sivota

Mainland Greece: Ioannina and Meteora

Mount Olympus and Dion

Acheron River and Necromanteion

Chapter 11
Itineraries and Sample Plans

Weekend Getaway

Cultural Immersion

Outdoor Adventure

Family-Friendly Trip

Budget Travel

Chapter 12
Safety Tips and Guidelines in Corfu

Sun Protection and Hydration

Water Safety and Beach Precautions

Beach Safety Measures

Safety Recommendations for Crime and Personal Security

Crime Prevention

Emergency Services and Healthcare Facilities

Emergency Services

Medical Facilities

Wildlife and Environmental Risks

Guidance for Solo Travelers and Families

Families

Conclusion

Chapter 13
Cultural Etiquette and Customs in Corfu

Attire Guidelines and Modesty Considerations

Greetings and Social Etiquette

Tipping Practices and Service Standards

Adherence to Local Customs and Traditions

Photography Guidelines in Corfu

Language Assistance and Basic Greek Phrases

In Conclusion

Chapter 14
Dos and don'ts in Corfu

Respect for Local Traditions and Customs

Environmental Conservation Practices

Appropriate Conduct at Archaeological Sites

Interaction with Wildlife and Marine Life

Safety Measures for Outdoor Activities

Principles of Responsible Tourism

Conclusion and Farewell

Corfu's Key Highlights in Summary

Final Advice for Visitors

A Fond Farewell from the Author

Corfu Glossary

Chapter 15
Appendix: Useful Resources

Emergency Contacts

Maps and Navigational Tools

Additional Reading and References

Useful Local Phrases

Website Links

Addresses and Locations of Popular Accommodation

Luxury Resorts

Budget-Friendly Hotels

Boutique Guesthouses

Unique Stays

Addresses and Locations of Popular Restaurants and Cafés

Restaurants
Cafés

Addresses and Locations of Popular Bars and Clubs

Bars

Clubs

Addresses and Locations of Top Attractions

INTRODUCTION

WELCOME TO CORFU, GREECE!

Greetings, fellow traveler, and welcome to the stunning island of Corfu! Nestled in the Ionian Sea, just off Greece's northwest coast, Corfu is a true Mediterranean jewel. Allow me to guide you through this captivating island, where history, culture, and natural beauty effortlessly intertwine to offer an unforgettable experience.

Welcome to Corfu

As you arrive in Corfu, you'll be embraced by the warm Mediterranean breeze, the fragrant scent of olive groves, and the inviting azure waters gently caressing the coastline. The island's lively atmosphere and relaxed charm will immediately engage your senses, promising a journey filled with discovery and relaxation.

Brief Overview of Corfu

Corfu, also known as Kerkyra in Greek, is the second-largest island in the Ionian Sea, with a history that stretches back thousands of years. Its strategic location has drawn settlers and conquerors throughout history, leaving behind a rich legacy of diverse cultures and architectural styles. From ancient Greek temples and Venetian fortresses to British colonial mansions, Corfu's heritage is as varied as its breathtaking landscapes.

Why Visit Corfu?

So, why should you choose Corfu as your next destination? The island has something for everyone.

Whether you're a history enthusiast, a nature lover, a food aficionado, or simply seeking relaxation on sun-soaked beaches, Corfu has it all.

The island's charming villages, lush green hills, and crystal-clear waters provide the perfect setting for a memorable holiday.

Tips for Visitors

Before you set off on your Corfu adventure, here are a few tips to enhance your visit:

Currency: The official currency is the Euro (EUR), so it's handy to have some cash for small purchases.

Language: While Greek is the official language, English is widely spoken, especially in tourist areas.

Transportation: Renting a car or scooter is a great way to explore the island at your own pace. Alternatively, public buses and taxis are available for getting around.

Weather: Corfu enjoys a Mediterranean climate with hot, dry summers and mild, wet winters. Remember to pack sunscreen, a hat, and plenty of water, especially during the summer.

Respect Local Customs: Dress modestly when visiting churches and monasteries, and always ask for permission before taking photos of locals.

About This Guide

In this guide, I will act as your personal tour guide, offering insider tips, uncovering hidden gems, and pointing out must-see attractions to ensure you get the most out of your visit to Corfu.

Whether your interest lies in exploring ancient ruins, indulging in delectable Greek cuisine, or simply relaxing on sun-drenched beaches, this guide has you covered.

How to Use This Guide

To make the most of this guide, simply scroll through the various sections, each spotlighting Corfu's attractions, activities, dining options, and more. Every section includes detailed information and recommendations to help you plan your itinerary and create unforgettable memories on this enchanting island.

Are you ready to embark on an adventure of exploration and discovery in Corfu? Let's dive in and experience everything this mesmerizing island has to offer!

CHAPTER 1

GETTING TO KNOW CORFU

Hey there, fellow adventurer! Let's start our journey by delving into the enchanting island of Corfu. From its breathtaking landscapes to its rich history and vibrant culture, Corfu has so much to offer. So, grab a cup of Greek coffee, and let's dive in!

Corfu: An Island Overview

Imagine this: lush green hillsides adorned with olive groves, quaint villages with colorful houses, and pristine beaches kissed by turquoise waters. That's Corfu in a nutshell! Located in the Ionian Sea, off the northwest coast of Greece, Corfu is the second-largest Ionian Island and a true Mediterranean paradise. With its diverse landscapes, charming towns, and warm hospitality, Corfu has captured the hearts of travelers from around the globe.

Geography and Climate of Corfu

Let's talk geography. Corfu boasts a varied terrain, from rugged mountains in the interior to sandy beaches along the coastline. The island's Mediterranean climate means long, hot summers and mild winters, making it an ideal destination year-round. Whether you're wandering the winding streets of Corfu Town, hiking through the lush countryside, or lounging on the beach, you'll be greeted by breathtaking scenery at every turn.

Corfu's History and Culture

The history and culture of Corfu are as rich and diverse as its landscapes. Over the centuries, the island has been home to Greeks, Romans, Venetians, French, and British, each leaving their mark on its architecture, cuisine, and traditions. From ancient Greek temples and Byzantine churches to Venetian fortresses and British colonial mansions, Corfu's heritage is a fascinating tapestry of influences. Make sure to explore the UNESCO-listed Old Town of Corfu, where narrow alleys, Venetian-style buildings, and charming squares transport you back in time.

Language and Communication

Let's discuss language. While Greek is the official language of Corfu, you'll find that many locals also speak English, especially in tourist areas. So, don't worry if your Greek is a bit rusty – you'll have no trouble communicating with the friendly locals. Of course, it never hurts to learn a few basic phrases like "kalimera" (good morning), "efharisto" (thank you), and "parakalo" (please), which will surely earn you a smile or two.

Navigating the Island

So, how do you get around Corfu? Well, there are plenty of options to suit every traveler's needs. If you're feeling adventurous, renting a car or scooter is a great way to explore the island at your own pace. Just be prepared for narrow roads and winding mountain paths! If you prefer to let someone else do the driving, you can hop on a local bus or taxi to get around. And for those who want to take to the water, there are boat tours and ferries to nearby islands like Paxos and Antipaxos.

As you can see, Corfu is a magical destination just waiting to be explored. So, pack your bags, grab your camera, and get ready for an adventure of a lifetime on this beautiful island!

CHAPTER 2

PLANNING YOUR TRIP TO CORFU

Welcome to the thrilling phase of planning your unforgettable journey to the enchanting island of Corfu! Let's dive into the details of organizing your trip to ensure everything goes smoothly, from selecting the best time to visit to navigating the island's transportation options and choosing the perfect accommodation to match your preferences and needs.

Best Time to Visit Corfu

Choosing the optimal time to visit Corfu is crucial for a successful trip. The island enjoys a Mediterranean climate with long, sunny summers and mild, wet winters, offering different experiences depending on the season. The peak tourist period is from June to August, characterized by lively energy, bustling beaches, and warm temperatures perfect for soaking up the Mediterranean sun. However, if you prefer a quieter escape with fewer crowds and lower accommodation costs, consider visiting during the shoulder seasons of spring (April to May) or fall (September to October). During these times, you can enjoy mild temperatures, blooming flora, and the tranquility of Corfu's landscapes.

How to Get to Corfu

Let's map out our route to this island paradise. Corfu is easily accessible via Corfu International Airport, also known as Ioannis Kapodistrias Airport, which receives domestic and international flights from major European cities. Upon arrival, you'll find yourself a short drive away from Corfu Town, the island's vibrant capital. There are plenty of transportation options from the airport to your accommodation, including taxis, buses, and rental cars, ensuring a smooth start to your Corfu adventure.

Transportation on the Island

Once you've arrived on Corfu's shores, getting around the island's diverse landscapes is straightforward. Whether you're exploring the historic streets of Corfu Town, embarking on a scenic drive through the lush countryside, or heading to secluded beaches along the coastline, there are transportation options to suit every traveler's needs. Renting a car or scooter offers the freedom to explore

Corfu at your own pace, uncovering hidden gems and stunning views along the way. Alternatively, the island's efficient public bus system connects major towns and attractions, providing a convenient and budget-friendly mode of transportation. For a hassle-free journey, taxis are readily available and offer a comfortable way to navigate the island's terrain.

Where to Stay in Corfu

Selecting the ideal lodging is crucial for an unforgettable stay in Corfu. The island offers a wide range of accommodation options, from luxurious resorts along the coast to quaint boutique hotels in historic villages. If you're drawn to the allure of beachfront living, coastal resorts invite you with their pristine sands, crystal-clear waters, and top-notch amenities. For those seeking cultural immersion, boutique hotels in Corfu Town offer charm and elegance, providing easy access to historic landmarks, lively markets, and authentic dining experiences. Meanwhile, travelers yearning for a peaceful retreat amidst nature will find comfort in countryside villas and rustic guesthouses, offering panoramic views and warm hospitality.

Choosing Your Accommodation

When searching for the perfect place to stay in Corfu, consider a few key factors to guide your decision. Location significantly impacts your experience—decide whether you prefer the tranquility of a secluded beach or the vibrant activity of Corfu Town. Evaluate the amenities each accommodation offers, from refreshing pools and rejuvenating spas to exquisite dining options and free Wi-Fi. Consider the ambiance and atmosphere of each establishment, ensuring it aligns with your travel style and preferences. Reading traveler reviews and recommendations can provide valuable insights and help you choose an accommodation that meets your expectations, ensuring a memorable and fulfilling stay in Corfu.

Accessibility and Special Needs

Ensuring inclusivity and accessibility is essential for a welcoming travel experience in Corfu. The island strives to cater to travelers with special needs or mobility issues, with many hotels, restaurants, and attractions featuring wheelchair access and other facilities to enhance accessibility. Transportation services, including taxis and buses, aim to accommodate diverse needs, ensuring all visitors can explore the island's wonders comfortably. If you have specific requirements or preferences, communicate them with your accommodation or tour provider in advance, allowing them to tailor their services to meet your needs and ensure a seamless and enjoyable experience throughout your stay in Corfu.

With these insights and considerations, you're well-prepared to embark on your journey to Corfu, filled with anticipation and excitement for the adventures ahead. So pack your bags, plan your itinerary, and get ready to immerse yourself in the unparalleled beauty and charm of this Mediterranean paradise!

CHAPTER 3

ACCOMMODATION OPTIONS IN CORFU

Ah, discovering the ideal accommodation in Corfu is like unearthing a hidden gem amidst the island's lush landscapes and azure seas. With a wide range of options to suit every traveler's taste and budget, let me guide you through the enchanting world of Corfu's lodging choices, from opulent resorts to charming boutique guesthouses and everything in between.

Overview of Accommodation Options

Corfu boasts a variety of lodging options, each with its own unique charm and appeal. Whether you're looking for ultimate luxury, a budget-friendly escape, or a quaint guesthouse steeped in local hospitality, there's something to satisfy every desire.

Luxury Resorts

For those seeking the height of indulgence and relaxation, Corfu's luxury resorts offer opulent amenities, exceptional service, and stunning views. Here are five top luxury resorts in Corfu:

1. Ikos Dassia

Location: Dassia, Corfu

Address: Dassia, 49100, Greece

Description: Located along the pristine shores of Dassia Beach, Ikos Dassia offers an unparalleled all-inclusive experience with stylish accommodations, gourmet dining options, and a variety of recreational activities.

2. MarBella Corfu

Location: Agios Ioannis Peristeron, Corfu

Address: Agios Ioannis Peristeron, 49084, Greece

Description: Set amidst lush gardens overlooking the Ionian Sea, MarBella Corfu is a luxurious beachfront retreat featuring elegant rooms, exquisite dining venues, and a world-class spa.

3. Grecotel Corfu Imperial

Location: Kommeno, Corfu

Address: Kommeno, 49100, Greece

Description: Situated on a private peninsula with views of the azure Ionian Sea, Grecotel Corfu Imperial provides a secluded sanctuary of luxury and tranquility, complete with private beaches, gourmet restaurants, and lavish accommodations.

4. Domes Miramare, a Luxury Collection Resort

Location: Moraitika, Corfu

Address: Moraitika, 49084, Greece

Description: Once the private retreat of the Greek royal family, Domes Miramare is a timeless haven of elegance and sophistication, featuring luxurious suites, fine dining establishments, and a serene spa overlooking the sea.

5. Corfu Holiday Palace

Location: Kanoni, Corfu

Address: Kanoni, 49100, Greece

Description: Located on a verdant hillside overlooking the iconic Mouse Island, Corfu Holiday Palace offers panoramic views of the Ionian Sea, luxurious accommodations, gourmet dining, and a range of recreational facilities.

Budget-Friendly Hotels

Travelers on a budget will find plenty of affordable accommodations in Corfu without sacrificing comfort or convenience. Here are five top budget-friendly hotels in Corfu:

1. Sunflower Apartments

Location: Sidari, Corfu

Address: Sidari, 49081, Greece

Description: Situated in the lively resort town of Sidari, Sunflower Apartments offer comfortable and affordable accommodations within walking distance of the beach, shops, and restaurants.

2. Benitses Arches

Location: Benitses, Corfu

Address: Benitses, 49084, Greece

Description: Located in the charming village of Benitses, Benitses Arches provides cozy rooms and studios at budget-friendly prices, just a short stroll from the beach and local tavernas.

3. Angelina Hotel & Apartments

Location: Gouvia, Corfu

Address: Gouvia, 49100, Greece

Description: Nestled amidst lush gardens in the resort town of Gouvia, Angelina Hotel & Apartments offer comfortable accommodations with easy access to the beach, shops, and nightlife.

4. Elena Hotel

Location: Kavos, Corfu

Address: Kavos, 49080, Greece

Description: Located in the bustling resort town of Kavos, Elena Hotel provides simple yet cozy accommodations just steps away from the beach, restaurants, and bars.

5. Margarita Beach Hotel

Location: Agios Gordios, Corfu

Address: Agios Gordios, 49084, Greece

Description: Set amidst olive groves overlooking Agios Gordios Beach, Margarita Beach Hotel offers affordable rooms and apartments with stunning sea views and easy access to the village center.

Boutique Guesthouses

For those who prefer a more intimate and personalized stay, Corfu's boutique guesthouses offer a delightful mix of local charm and unique accommodations. Here are five top boutique guesthouses in Corfu:

1. Villa Kapella

Location: Lakones, Corfu

Address: Lakones, 49083, Greece

Description: Nestled on a hillside with panoramic views of the Ionian Sea, Villa Kapella provides cozy rooms and apartments overlooking the picturesque village of Lakones.

2. Cavalieri Hotel

Location: Corfu Town, Corfu

Address: 4 Capodistriou Street, Corfu Town, 49100, Greece

Description: Situated in a 17th-century Venetian mansion in central Corfu Town, Cavalieri Hotel offers elegant accommodations, personalized service, and a rooftop terrace with stunning views of the Old Fortress and the sea.

3. Mayor Mon Repos Palace Art Hotel

Location: Corfu Town, Corfu

Address: Dimokratias Avenue, Corfu Town, 49100, Greece

Description: Located amidst lush gardens overlooking Garitsa Bay, Mayor Mon Repos Palace Art Hotel combines historic charm with modern amenities, offering stylish rooms and suites with sea views and access to a private beach.

4. Arcadion Hotel

Location: Corfu Town, Corfu

Address: 2 Vlassopoulou Street, Corfu Town, 49100, Greece

Description: Set in the heart of Corfu Town's historic center, Arcadion Hotel offers boutique accommodations blending traditional elegance with modern comfort, just steps away from shops, restaurants, and attractions.

5. Locandiera Guesthouse

Location: Old Perithia, Corfu

Address: Old Perithia, 49081, Greece

Description: Hidden in the charming mountain village of Old Perithia, Locandiera Guesthouse features rustic-chic accommodations in a historic stone building, surrounded by pristine nature and hiking trails.

Unique Stays

For an unforgettable and unique experience, Corfu offers a selection of distinctive accommodations that promise to leave a lasting impression. Here are five top unique stays in Corfu:

1. Aquis Agios Gordios Beach Hotel

Location: Agios Gordios, Corfu

Address: Agios Gordios, 49084, Greece

Description: Located on the beachfront in Agios Gordios, Aquis Agios Gordios Beach Hotel offers stylish accommodations in a modern setting, with direct access to the beach and stunning sea views.

2. Cavo Bianco

Location: Barbati, Corfu

Address: Barbati, 49083, Greece

Description: Overlooking Barbati Beach, Cavo Bianco offers luxury suites and villas with private pools, personalized service, and panoramic views of the Ionian Sea.

3. Bella Mare Hotel

Location: Agios Spyridon, Corfu

Address: Agios Spyridon, 49081, Greece

Description: Situated near the village of Agios Spyridon, Bella Mare Hotel offers charming bungalows and studios with traditional décor, a swimming pool, and a cozy taverna serving homemade Greek cuisine.

4. San Antonio Corfu Resort

Location: Kalami, Corfu

Address: Kalami, 49083, Greece

Description: Nestled on a secluded beach in Kalami Bay, San Antonio Corfu Resort features luxurious suites and villas with private pools, beachfront dining, and exclusive access to a pristine stretch of coastline.

5. Gelina Village & Aqua Park

Location: Acharavi, Corfu

Address: Acharavi, 49081, Greece

Description: Ideal for families and fun-seekers, Gelina Village & Aqua Park offers comfortable accommodations, a water park with slides and pools, and a variety of activities and entertainment for guests of all ages.

Top Recommended Hotels and Resorts

After exploring the diverse accommodation options in Corfu, a few establishments stand out for their exceptional service, stunning locations, and rave reviews from travelers. Here are five top recommended hotels and resorts in Corfu:

1. Ikos Dassia

Location: Dassia, Corfu

Address: Dassia, 49100, Greece

Description: Known for its impeccable service, luxurious amenities, and stunning beachfront location, Ikos Dassia consistently ranks among the top resorts in Corfu, offering an unforgettable all-inclusive experience.

2. MarBella Corfu

Location: Agios Ioannis Peristeron, Corfu

Address: Agios Ioannis Peristeron, 49084, Greece

Description: Famous for its exquisite dining, elegant accommodations, and breathtaking sea views, MarBella

Corfu is a perennial favorite among travelers seeking a luxurious beachfront escape.

3. Villa Kapella

Location: Lakones, Corfu

Address: Lakones, 49083, Greece

Description: With its panoramic views, cozy accommodations, and warm hospitality, Villa Kapella offers a quintessential Corfu experience in the picturesque village of Lakones.

4. Cavalieri Hotel

Location: Corfu Town, Corfu

Address: 4 Capodistriou Street, Corfu Town, 49100, Greece

Description: Set in a historic Venetian mansion, Cavalieri Hotel exudes old-world charm and sophistication, providing guests with an elegant and memorable stay in the heart of Corfu Town.

5. Sunflower Apartments

Location: Sidari, Corfu

Address: Sidari, 49081, Greece

Description: Offering comfortable accommodations and a warm, family-friendly atmosphere, Sunflower Apartments is a top choice for budget-conscious travelers seeking a cozy retreat near Sidari's bustling beaches and nightlife.

Choosing the Right Accommodation for You

When selecting the perfect place to stay in Corfu, consider key factors to ensure a memorable experience. Reflect on your preferences regarding location, amenities, and ambiance. Whether you crave the luxury of a beachfront resort, the charm of a boutique guesthouse, or the affordability of a budget-friendly hotel, choose the accommodation that resonates with your travel style and aspirations.

Booking Tips and Tricks

As you book your accommodation in Corfu, keep these tips in mind to secure the best deals and ensure a seamless experience:

Book Early: To get the best rates and availability, book your accommodation well in advance, especially during peak seasons.

Compare Prices: Check multiple booking platforms to compare prices and find the best deals.

Read Reviews: Read reviews and testimonials from other travelers to understand the quality and experience of each accommodation.

Consider Package Deals: Some resorts and hotels offer package deals that include accommodations, meals, and activities, providing excellent value and simplifying your planning.

Flexible Dates: If possible, be flexible with your travel dates to take advantage of lower rates and special offers during off-peak seasons.

Armed with these tips, you're ready to navigate the world of accommodation booking in Corfu and secure the perfect retreat for your Mediterranean adventure. So go ahead, dream big, and book your slice of paradise in this enchanting island oasis!

CHAPTER 4

EXPLORING CORFU TOWN

Corfu Town – a maze of winding alleys, ancient fortresses, and Venetian allure awaits those willing to explore its ageless charm. Join me as we uncover the secrets of this cultural center, from its lively port and waterfront to its fascinating museums, bustling markets, and delightful dining scene. Let's delve into the essence of Corfu Town and discover its hidden gems together!

Corfu Town: A Cultural Hub

Corfu Town, also known as Kerkyra, is the vibrant capital of the island, woven with a rich history, culture, and architecture. Its UNESCO-listed Old Town, imposing fortresses, and bustling squares make Corfu Town a living museum waiting to be explored. Lose yourself in its twisting streets, where Byzantine churches stand alongside

Venetian mansions, and ancient ruins whisper tales from centuries ago.

Corfu Port and Waterfront

Our adventure begins at the bustling port of Corfu Town, where ferries and cruise ships arrive daily, bringing a steady stream of travelers eager to explore the island's wonders. Take a leisurely stroll along the waterfront promenade, where colorful fishing boats bob in the harbor, and waterfront cafes call out with their enticing appeal. Admire the commanding silhouette of the Old Fortress, which guards the entrance to the port, and marvel at the panoramic views of the Ionian Sea stretching out before you.

Museums and Historical Sites

Corfu Town is a treasure trove of museums and historical sites, each offering a glimpse into the island's rich heritage and storied past. Visit the Archaeological Museum of Corfu, which houses a captivating collection of artifacts spanning thousands of years, from ancient Greek pottery to Roman sculptures. Wander through the halls of the Museum of Asian Art, set in a beautiful neoclassical mansion, and marvel at its impressive collection of Chinese, Japanese, and Indian art.

Local Markets and Shopping

No visit to Corfu Town is complete without exploring its lively markets and shopping streets, where you can immerse yourself in the vibrant sights, sounds, and scents of local life. Browse the bustling stalls of the Municipal Market, where vendors sell fresh produce, seafood, and spices, or wander the cobblestone streets of the Old Town, where boutiques and artisan workshops offer unique wares. Be sure to pick up a bottle of Corfu's famous kumquat liqueur as a memento of your adventures!

Dining and Cuisine in Corfu Town

After a day of exploring, delight your palate with the culinary wonders of Corfu Town's vibrant dining scene. From traditional Greek tavernas serving moussaka and souvlaki to chic rooftop restaurants offering panoramic city views, there's something to please every taste. Indulge in fresh seafood caught from the Ionian Sea, savor local specialties like pastitsada and bourdeto, and pair it all with a glass of crisp white wine from the island's vineyards.

Nightlife and Entertainment Options

As the sun sets over Corfu Town, the city transforms into a vibrant nightlife scene, catering to every taste and mood. Enjoy cocktails at a waterfront bar with live music, dance the night away at a lively nightclub, or simply wander the moonlit streets, soaking in the ambiance of this enchanting city. For those seeking traditional Greek culture, don't miss a live performance of music and dance at one of the many tavernas scattered throughout the Old Town.

Conclusion

Corfu Town is a city of contrasts, where ancient history meets modern charm, and every corner holds a new discovery. From its historic landmarks and cultural attractions to its lively markets, dining scene, and nightlife options, there's no shortage of things to see and do here. So lace up your walking shoes, grab your camera, and prepare to be captivated by the timeless beauty of Corfu Town – a city that will steal your heart and leave you yearning to return again and again.

CHAPTER 5

TOP TOURIST ATTRACTIONS IN CORFU

Step into the enchanting realm of Corfu's most captivating sights, where ancient tales, natural splendor, and architectural marvels beckon at every twist and turn. Let's embark on a journey to uncover the essence of this mesmerizing island, from the majestic palaces and fortresses to the sun-kissed beaches and charming villages that adorn its shores.

Achilleion Palace

Our voyage commences at the magnificent Achilleion Palace, a tribute to the grandeur of Greece's imperial legacy. Perched atop the glistening waters of the Ionian Sea, this lavish palace once served as the summer retreat for Empress Elisabeth of Austria, also known as Sisi. Immerse yourself in history as you traverse its richly embellished chambers, adorned with murals, sculptures, and intricate furnishings. Be sure not to overlook the iconic statue of Achilles gracing the palace gardens, gazing stoically towards the sea, or the panoramic vistas of Corfu's coastline from the palace terraces.

Old Fortress of Corfu

Our next destination is the iconic Old Fortress of Corfu, a formidable bastion of stone that has stood sentinel over the city for ages. Dating back to the 6th century AD, this imposing fortress offers insight into Corfu's tumultuous past, from Byzantine dominion to Venetian rule and beyond. Ascend its ancient ramparts for sweeping vistas of the city below, navigate its labyrinthine passages and chambers, and envisage the conflicts that once echoed within its walls. Don't miss the opportunity to visit the Old Fortress's lighthouse at dusk, when the sky ignites with fiery hues and the sea glimmers in the fading light – a spectacle not to be missed.

Liston Promenade

As dusk descends, we venture to the Liston Promenade, a graceful arcade flanked by chic cafes and eateries. Constructed during the French occupation of Corfu in the 19th century, this iconic promenade is an ideal spot to unwind and absorb the city's ambiance. Take a leisurely stroll beneath its shaded colonnades, savor a glass of ouzo at a sidewalk cafe, and observe life unfold as locals and visitors mingle in this timeless locale. With luck, you may chance upon a traditional Corfiot band serenading folk tunes in the square – a magical encounter that transports you through time.

Paleokastritsa Monastery

Our odyssey leads us to the serene shores of Paleokastritsa, home to one of Corfu's holiest sites – the Paleokastritsa Monastery. Nestled amid verdant hills overlooking the azure expanse of the Ionian Sea, this Byzantine monastery exudes tranquility and spirituality. Explore its ornate chapel adorned with frescoes and icons dating back to the 13th century, and wander through its serene gardens, where fragrant blooms and ancient olive trees stand sentinel. Take a moment to pause and contemplate in the monastery's courtyard, where the chants of monks mingle with the gentle lapping of waves below – an ethereal experience that lingers long after departing its sacred precincts.

Sidari Beach and Canal d'Amour

No excursion to Corfu would be complete without a sojourn to the idyllic shores of Sidari, where sun, sand, and romance await at every turn. Bask in the golden sunshine as you recline upon the powdery sands of Sidari Beach, or indulge in a revitalizing swim in the crystalline waters of the Ionian Sea. And be sure to explore the renowned Canal d'Amour,

CHAPTER 6

OUTDOOR ACTIVITIES IN CORFU

The endless marvels of Corfu's great outdoors beckon us, where the gentle rustle of winds through ancient olive groves and the glistening expanse of the Ionian Sea invite exploration. Join me on a journey through the array of outdoor pursuits that this captivating island boasts. From invigorating hikes through lush forests to serene horseback rides along pristine beaches, Corfu is a sanctuary for adventurers and nature enthusiasts alike.

Hiking and Nature Trails

Corfu's rugged terrains present a haven for hikers, boasting a vast network of trails meandering through verdant forests, charming villages, and rugged mountainsides. Equip yourself with sturdy footwear and venture forth to uncover the island's natural splendor, where each step reveals a new marvel. The Corfu Trail, a picturesque path spanning the island's length, offers awe-inspiring vistas of the Ionian Sea and the verdant countryside. Along the way, encounter hidden waterfalls cascading into crystalline pools, ancient ruins steeped in history, and fragrant wildflowers blooming profusely. Allow the tranquility of nature to embrace you as you navigate the rugged landscapes, immersing yourself in the beauty of Corfu's wilderness.

Watersports and Beach Activities

With its azure waters and sun-kissed shores, Corfu emerges as a paradise for water sports enthusiasts of all ages.

Plunge into the sparkling sea and partake in an array of aquatic adventures, from snorkeling and scuba diving to windsurfing and jet skiing.

Explore concealed coves and underwater caverns, where vibrant coral reefs teem with marine life, and frolic alongside playful dolphins and graceful sea turtles.

For those seeking an adrenaline surge, consider trying parasailing or wakeboarding. With rental facilities and water sports centers dotting the coastline, opportunities abound to revel in Corfu's crystalline waters.

After a day of aquatic excitement, unwind on the sandy expanses of one of Corfu's myriad beaches, where you can soak up the sun, savor a refreshing beverage, and observe life's ebb and flow.

Cycling and Biking Routes

For those inclined towards leisurely exploration, Corfu presents a network of cycling and biking routes winding through olive groves, vineyards, and picturesque countryside. Pedal along coastal paths and rural lanes, pausing to admire ancient ruins, Byzantine churches, and panoramic vistas en route. The Corfu Mountain Bike Park beckons mountain biking enthusiasts with trails catering to various skill levels. From gentle slopes to challenging descents, there exists a route tailored for everyone's enjoyment. With bike rental facilities conveniently dispersed across the island, embarking on a cycling adventure to uncover Corfu's hidden gems at your own pace is effortlessly achievable.

Boat Tours and Excursions

Embark on a maritime escapade and explore Corfu's coastline from the deck of a boat, yacht, or kayak. Glide across the shimmering expanse of the Ionian Sea, making pit stops to swim in secluded coves, snorkel over vibrant reefs, and bask on sandy shores. Discover clandestine sea caves and coastal grottoes, where ancient myths and legends come alive, or embark on a sunset voyage and witness the sky ablaze with fiery hues. From leisurely sailboats to high-speed catamarans, an array of boat tours and excursions caters to every preference in Corfu. Seize the opportunity to visit neighboring islands such as Paxos and Antipaxos, where quaint villages, delectable cuisine, and the unhurried island lifestyle await exploration.

Fishing and Snorkeling Spots

For anglers and underwater enthusiasts, Corfu presents an array of fishing and snorkeling sites awaiting discovery. Cast your line from rocky shores, sandy beaches, or traditional fishing vessels, reeling in a plethora of fresh seafood, from succulent sea bass to plump octopus. Alternatively, don your snorkeling gear and plunge into the crystalline depths of the Ionian Sea, where vibrant reefs and submerged caves beckon. Swim alongside shoals of fish, spot elusive seahorses, and marvel at the myriad marine species inhabiting Corfu's coastal waters. Whether a novice angler or seasoned snorkeler, Corfu offers ample opportunities to commune with nature and behold the enchantment of its underwater realm.

Engage in horseback riding and equestrian pursuits to traverse Corfu's countryside, where ancient paths and picturesque routes unveil the island's allure from a distinct vantage point. Participate in guided horseback excursions, meandering along sandy shores, meandering woodland tracks, and sunlit vineyards, pausing to appreciate sweeping vistas of the Ionian Sea. For enthusiasts of equestrian sports, consider trying your hand at disciplines like show jumping, dressage, or even polo at one of Corfu's equestrian facilities. Whether a seasoned equestrian or a novice rider, there's a certain enchantment to exploring the island on horseback, as the rhythmic cadence of hooves guides you through the serene countryside.

As our exploration of Corfu's outdoor pursuits draws to a close, I trust you've been inspired to delve into the splendor and excitement awaiting on this captivating island. Whether trekking through verdant forests, plunging into crystalline waters, or journeying by horseback along the coast, Corfu offers boundless avenues for exploration and communion with nature. So pack your adventurous spirit, embrace the allure of discovery, and prepare to craft enduring memories in this picturesque corner of Greece.

CHAPTER 7

CULTURAL EXPERIENCES IN CORFU

Welcome to the epicenter of Corfu's dynamic cultural milieu, where age-old customs seamlessly merge with contemporary influences, offering a mosaic of diverse and enriching encounters. Join me as we delve into the essence of this captivating island, immersing ourselves in its timeless traditions, artistic expressions, and gastronomic pleasures.

Traditional Greek Festivals and Events

Corfu is renowned for its vibrant festivals and events, which pay homage to the island's rich cultural legacy and strong sense of community. From religious processions to folk music concerts, the streets of Corfu are always abuzz with activity. Among the most renowned festivities is the Easter celebration, where the island bursts with colorful parades, solemn processions, and traditional banquets. Equally captivating is the Corfu Carnival, a lively spectacle preceding Lent, marked by masked revelers, exuberant costumes, and spirited music, as locals and visitors alike revel in dance, song, and the heralding of spring. Notable events include the Feast of St. Spyridon, patron saint of Corfu, and the Corfu Beer Festival, offering a taste of locally brewed beers and authentic Greek fare.

Local Arts and Crafts Workshops

Uncover the artistic flair of Corfu and delve into the island's thriving arts and crafts community. From pottery to painting, weaving to sculpture, a wealth of talent awaits discovery.

Explore local workshops and studios to witness skilled artisans employing traditional methods passed down through generations.

Delve into the history and significance of each craft, from the intricate motifs of Byzantine iconography to the vivid hues of Venetian glassblowing.

Engage in hands-on workshops and classes tailored to all skill levels, offering a chance to create your own masterpiece.

Whether drawn to traditional folk art or contemporary design, Corfu provides a unique opportunity to connect with local creatives and bolster the island's artistic legacy.

Cooking Classes and Culinary Tours

Awaken your senses and embark on a gastronomic odyssey through the flavors of Corfu. From aromatic herbs to succulent seafood, the island's cuisine celebrates local ingredients and time-honored recipes. Enroll in a cooking class to master traditional Greek dishes, from moussaka to baklava, sourcing fresh produce from local markets and olive groves. Alternatively, culinary tours offer a tantalizing array of local delicacies, from meze platters to homemade pastries, complemented by regional wines. Whether a culinary novice or seasoned epicurean, Corfu's culinary offerings are certain to tantalize your taste buds and leave you yearning for more.

Music and Dance Performances

Immerse yourself in the rhythm and vitality of Greek music and dance with captivating live performances and traditional entertainment.

From bouzouki melodies to syrtaki rhythms, Corfu's cultural scene comes alive after sundown. Gather at local tavernas or outdoor amphitheaters for an evening of music, dance, and revelry, as talented musicians and dancers take center stage.

Whether joining in traditional Greek dances like the kalamatiano or simply tapping along to the beat, the music of Corfu embodies the island's diverse cultural heritage and spirited ethos, leaving you uplifted and inspired.

Religious Observances and Pilgrimages

Corfu's religious customs are deeply ingrained in its past and present, featuring a diverse array of ceremonies and observances passed down over generations. From ancient Byzantine churches to Venetian chapels, the island is adorned with sacred spaces that foster spiritual contemplation and communal gatherings. Join the faithful in religious processions, pilgrimages, and festivals honoring the island's patron saints and revered icons. Among the most venerated figures is St. Spyridon, whose relics rest in the magnificent St. Spyridon Church in Corfu Town's heart. Annually, thousands of pilgrims converge upon the church to pay homage to the saint, seeking blessings for well-being, prosperity, and safeguarding. Whether devout or simply intrigued by the island's religious heritage, Corfu presents a remarkable opportunity to witness the fusion of faith and culture in an enchanting ambiance.

Cultural Heritage Conservation Endeavors

Preserving Corfu's cultural legacy is a heartfelt endeavor, championed by devoted individuals and organizations committed to safeguarding the island's traditions, landmarks, and historical treasures. From refurbishing ancient monuments to archiving oral narratives, these endeavors ensure the transmission of Corfu's rich cultural heritage to future generations. Explore museums, libraries, and cultural hubs to delve into Corfu's captivating past and embrace its diverse cultural legacy. Extend support to local initiatives and conservation endeavors aimed at preserving and promoting the island's distinct identity and customs. Whether volunteering time, contributing funds, or raising awareness, every endeavor contributes to the enduring vitality of Corfu's cultural heritage.

As our exploration of Corfu's cultural tapestry draws to a close, I trust you've been inspired to delve deeper into the island's rich spectrum of traditions, artistic expressions, and gastronomic wonders. Whether partaking in local festivities, honing a craft in a traditional workshop, or savoring the flavors of Greek cuisine, Corfu promises an abundance of cultural encounters awaiting discovery. So, embrace your curiosity, embrace the spirit of exploration, and prepare to forge memories that will linger in your heart for years to come in this captivating corner of Greece.

CHAPTER 8

DINING AND CUISINE IN CORFU

Ah, the alluring scents of Greek cooking fill the air, inviting us to embark on a gastronomic voyage through Corfu's flavors. Come along as we traverse the island's lively dining landscape, where age-old recipes, fresh produce, and genuine hospitality blend to craft unforgettable culinary encounters.

Authentic Greek Tavernas and Eateries

Step into the cozy ambiance of a traditional Greek taverna and prepare to indulge in a medley of flavors celebrating Mediterranean cuisine's richness. Whether family-owned joints or seaside diners, Corfu boasts charming restaurants offering genuine Greek fare prepared with affection. Begin your feast with a mezze platter of tzatziki, hummus, and dolmades, followed by beloved classics like moussaka, souvlaki, and spanakopita. Save room for dessert, as no Greek meal is complete without baklava or creamy Greek yogurt drizzled with honey. Accompany your meal with ouzo or retsina, and linger over animated conversations late into the night. Whether dining in Corfu Town or a quaint village, Greek hospitality infuses every meal with lasting memories.

Corfu's Seafood Delights

Blessed with pristine shores and bountiful waters, Corfu offers a paradise for seafood enthusiasts, presenting a plethora of fresh and flavorsome dishes showcasing the sea's bounty. From grilled sardines and octopus to fried calamari and shrimp saganaki, the island's seafood specialties delight the palate. Delve into traditional offerings like bourdeto, a zesty fish stew, or kakavia, a hearty seafood soup, relishing locally caught fish and shellfish's briny goodness. For the quintessential seaside dining experience, head to a waterfront taverna, where alfresco dining allows the waves to caress your feet as you savor the salty air. Whether enjoying a leisurely lunch or a romantic dinner, Corfu's seafood treasures promise to leave you yearning for more.

Local Delights and Desserts

Satiate your sweet cravings with Corfu's irresistible desserts and indigenous delicacies, steeped in history and bursting with flavor. From syrup-laden pastries to creamy confections, the island's desserts celebrate Mediterranean ingredients and culinary expertise. Indulge in loukoumades, fried dough balls soaked in honey and dusted with cinnamon, or galaktoboureko, a sumptuous custard pie ensconced in crisp phyllo pastry. For a savory bite, savor tiropita, a flaky cheese pie, or spanakopita, a spinach and feta pastry melting in your mouth. Don't forget to treat yourself to traditional Greek ice cream, boasting flavors from pistachio and almond to fig and honey. With each bite, you'll taste the dedication to preserving Corfu's culinary legacy for generations to come.

Olive Oil Tasting and Production

No Corfu visit is complete without encountering Greek olive oil, revered for its flavor and health benefits across centuries. Wander through the island's olive groves and presses, where ancient trees stand witness to time's passage and generations of artisans perpetuate olive oil's age-old tradition. Learn about olive harvesting and pressing, from hand-picking to cold-pressing to retain the oil's essence and nutrients. Sample a variety of extra virgin olive oils, each boasting its unique aroma, flavor, and peppery kick. From delicate and fruity to robust and pungent, Corfu's olive oils epitomize the island's agricultural heritage and dedication to sustainable farming practices. Stock up on your favorites to bring a taste of Corfu home and infuse your culinary creations with Mediterranean charm.

Wine and Ouzo Tastings

Toast to Greek winemaking prowess with a tasting journey through Corfu's vineyards. From crisp whites to robust reds, the island's wines reflect its terroir and climate, offering distinct flavors and aromas encapsulating the Mediterranean essence. Explore local wineries to sample indigenous grape varieties like Robola and Kefalotiri alongside international favorites such as Merlot and Chardonnay. Delve into winemaking intricacies, from grape cultivation to barrel aging, and uncover the narratives behind each bottle. And for a quintessential Greek experience, savor ouzo, an anise-flavored spirit cherished as an aperitif or digestif. Sip slowly, relishing its nuanced flavors as you toast Corfu's beauty and the joy of camaraderie.

Recommended Dining Experiences

For an unforgettable culinary adventure, venture beyond the usual haunts and seek out hidden gems showcasing Corfu's gastronomic treasures. Dine in a traditional kafeneio, where locals gather for robust Greek coffee and hearty breakfasts. Alternatively, visit a mountainside taverna for rustic charm and dishes crafted from locally sourced ingredients. Indulge in luxury by booking a table at Corfu's fine dining establishments, where Michelin-starred chefs craft innovative Mediterranean-inspired dishes. For a more immersive experience, enroll in a cooking class or culinary tour to learn Greek cuisine's secrets from local chefs and home cooks. Whether dining seaside or amid mountain vistas, Corfu's culinary offerings promise an abundance of savory experiences waiting to be savored.

As our culinary odyssey through Corfu's flavors draws to a close, may you be inspired to savor the island's rich culinary legacy. Whether relishing fresh seafood by the shore, indulging in sweet treats at a local patisserie, or raising a glass of ouzo to health and happiness, Corfu's dining experiences are certain to leave an indelible mark. So, pack your appetite, brace your taste buds for adventure, and prepare for a culinary journey sure to tantalize your senses and leave you with cherished memories for years to come.

CHAPTER 9

SHOPPING AND MARKETS IN CORFU

Oh, the delight of exploring Corfu's lively markets and quaint boutiques, where each corner holds a treasure waiting to be found. Come with me as we venture on a shopping escapade through the winding streets of Corfu, where local artisans, craftsmen, and merchants showcase their goods with pride and zeal.

Souvenir Shops and Gift Boutiques

No Corfu journey is truly complete without snagging a few souvenirs to commemorate your time on this captivating island. From quirky keepsakes to handcrafted gems, Corfu's souvenir shops and gift boutiques boast an extensive array of memorabilia to cater to every fancy and budget. Browse through shelves adorned with olive wood carvings, ceramic pottery, and traditional Greek attire, or grab a jar of local honey or a bottle of olive oil to take a slice of Corfu home with you. Remember to snag postcards, magnets, and other trinkets to reminisce about your Corfu adventures. Whether seeking unique jewelry or quirky novelties to recall your travels, Corfu's souvenir shops cater to all.

Local Crafts and Artisanal Offerings

Dive into Corfu's rich artistic tapestry and uncover the island's vibrant craft community, where skilled artisans and craftsmen fashion exquisite handmade treasures using age-old techniques passed through generations. Pay a visit to local workshops and studios to observe artisans at work, shaping marble, weaving textiles, and painting intricate designs on ceramics. From elaborately embroidered textiles to intricately carved wooden figurines, Corfu's crafts speak volumes about the island's ingenuity and artistry. Support local artists by acquiring their unique creations, whether it's a piece of blown glass or a hand-painted ceramic tile. With each purchase, you not only bring home a one-of-a-kind keepsake but also contribute to preserving Corfu's cultural legacy for posterity.

Fresh Produce Markets and Stalls

Immerse yourself in the lively ambiance of Corfu's bustling markets, where local farmers and producers converge to vend their fresh fruits, vegetables, and culinary delights. Stroll through stalls brimming with a kaleidoscope of produce, from luscious tomatoes and aromatic herbs to succulent oranges and plump olives. Sample freshly baked bread, artisanal cheeses, and homemade preserves, engaging in conversations with vendors to glean insights into Corfu's culinary traditions. Whether stocking up for a picnic or relishing the market's vibrant energy, Corfu's markets promise a sensory extravaganza not to be missed.

Traditional Greek Products

Indulge in retail therapy as you peruse the wealth of traditional Greek products that Corfu boasts. From fragrant herbs and spices to handwoven textiles and ceramics, the island teems with treasures awaiting discovery. Explore local shops and boutiques showcasing racks of embroidered attire, shelves of local wines and spirits, and showcases of handmade baubles and adornments. Sample an array of Greek delicacies, from feta cheese and Kalamata olives to baklava and loukoumades, and stock up on your preferred flavors to carry a taste of Corfu home. Whether seeking a distinctive keepsake or simply reveling in retail therapy, Corfu's traditional Greek products promise to delight the senses and leave you with enduring memories of your island sojourn.

Bargaining Tips and Tactics

Though bargaining isn't as customary in Corfu as in some locales, opportunities to haggle over prices, especially at markets and smaller shops, do arise. When bargaining, maintain politeness and respect, initiating with a warm greeting and a smile. Take your time to peruse and compare prices before making an offer, and be prepared to walk away if the price isn't satisfactory. Remember, bargaining is more about fostering rapport and forging a connection with the seller than securing the lowest price. Above all, relish the experience of bargaining like a local, and don't forget to enjoy yourself.

Food and Wine Souvenirs Shopping

No Corfu excursion would be complete without savoring the island's delectable culinary offerings and bringing home a taste of Greece to share with loved ones. Explore local markets and specialty food shops to amass Greek olives, olive oil, and honey, along with traditional confections like baklava and loukoumades. Don't overlook securing a bottle or two of local wine or ouzo for your dining pleasure or as thoughtful gifts for family and friends. For the ultimate epicurean memento, why not enroll in a cooking class and master the art of crafting your beloved Greek dishes? With a dash of planning and a dollop of culinary curiosity, you'll relish Corfu's flavors long after your journey ends.

As our shopping escapade in Corfu draws to a close, I hope you're inspired to explore the island's vibrant markets, charming boutiques, and hidden gems. Whether seeking the perfect keepsake or indulging in a spot of retail therapy, Corfu promises an array of shopping experiences ripe for discovery. So, pack your bags, don your walking shoes, and prepare for a shopping spree that will yield memories to cherish for years to come.

CHAPTER 10

DAY TRIPS AND EXCURSIONS FROM CORFU

Welcome to the world of discovery beyond Corfu's coastline, where each day trip offers a fresh adventure and an opportunity to uncover the hidden treasures of the Ionian Sea. Come along as we explore neighboring islands, ancient ruins, and charming towns, immersing ourselves in the region's rich history and natural splendor.

Paxos and Antipaxos Islands

Embark on a voyage across the glistening waters of the Ionian Sea to the captivating isles of Paxos and Antipaxos, where rugged cliffs, azure bays, and olive groves beckon. As we cruise along Corfu's coast, the salty breeze tousles our hair, and the sun dances on the waves, creating an aura of serenity. Our first destination is Gaios, Paxos's quaint harbor town, where pastel buildings adorn the waterfront, and bougainvillea cascades from terraces above. We wander through narrow streets, passing whitewashed churches and cozy cafes, pausing to admire local crafts and savor regional delicacies. Then, we hop on a boat to Antipaxos, a tiny paradise renowned for its sandy beaches and crystal-clear waters. Here, we wade into the shallows, feeling the soft sand beneath our feet and the cool embrace of the sea. As the sun dips below the horizon in a symphony of colors, we raise a toast to the allure of the Ionian Islands and the magic of our day trip to Paxos and Antipaxos.

Albania: Saranda and Butrint

Crossing into Albania, we embark on a voyage to Butrint, an ancient city designated as a UNESCO World Heritage Site, steeped in history and myth. Journeying through olive groves and rolling hills, the landscape transitions from rugged coastline to verdant countryside, punctuated by remnants of ancient civilizations. Arriving at Butrint, we step back in time to explore temples, Roman baths, and a medieval fortress, each relic bearing witness to centuries of history. From the acropolis, we survey Lake Butrint's serene waters, where swans glide gracefully and nature's symphony fills the air. After a day of exploration, we proceed to Saranda, a bustling port town nestled between mountains and sea. Here, we stroll along the waterfront, savoring fresh seafood and robust coffee, before bidding adieu to Albania and returning to Corfu, our hearts brimming with memories and our minds brimming with tales of antiquity.

Parga and Sivota

Nestled on the Greek mainland, just a short ferry ride from Corfu, lie the picturesque towns of Parga and Sivota, where rugged cliffs, verdant hills, and azure waters converge to form a scene of unparalleled beauty. We embark on a leisurely cruise across the Ionian Sea, the salty breeze caressing our skin and the sun illuminating our path. Upon reaching Parga, we're greeted by a kaleidoscope of homes cascading down to the sea, crowned by a medieval fortress perched atop a rocky outcrop. Wandering through cobbled streets adorned with tavernas and boutiques, we pause to soak in panoramic vistas of the Ionian Sea and nearby isles. Then, we board a boat to Sivota's secluded coves and hidden beaches, where we revel in crystalline waters and golden sands. As the day draws to a close, we raise a glass to the splendor of mainland Greece and the joys of exploration.

Mainland Greece: Ioannina and Meteora

Venturing inland, we set our sights on Ioannina, a historic city boasting Byzantine fortresses, Ottoman mosques, and serene lakeside promenades. Meandering through narrow lanes lined with stone dwellings and vibrant gardens, we pause to delve into the city's rich past at the Byzantine and

Ali Pasha Museums. Next, we journey to the awe-inspiring monasteries of Meteora, perched atop towering rock formations that seem to touch the heavens. Ascending winding mountain roads, we're treated to panoramic vistas of unparalleled beauty. Upon reaching Meteora, we ascend stone steps to explore ancient monasteries and churches, marveling at the solitude and spirituality that permeate these sacred grounds. As we gaze upon the valley below, we're humbled by the grandeur of this sacred place and grateful for the opportunity to experience its magic firsthand.

Mount Olympus and Dion

Embark on a pilgrimage to Mount Olympus, the mythical abode of ancient Greek gods and the highest peak in Greece. Winding our way up mountain paths, the air grows crisper, and the fragrance of pine fills our senses. Upon reaching the mountain's base, we don our hiking boots and set out on a journey through lush forests and alpine meadows, pausing to admire cascading waterfalls and sweeping vistas. Along the way, we're regaled with tales of Zeus, Hera, and legendary heroes who once roamed these storied slopes. After a day of exploration, we descend to Dion, an ancient city where archaeological excavations reveal a wealth of artifacts from classical antiquity. Roaming among temple ruins and amphitheaters, we're transported back in time, imagining life in this ancient metropolis. As the sun sets on our day trip to Mount Olympus and Dion, we reflect on the enduring allure of

Greek mythology and the timeless legacy of ancient Greece.

Acheron River and Necromanteion

Embark on a journey to the realm of the underworld as we explore the mystical Acheron River and the ancient site of Necromanteion, where ancient Greeks communed with the spirits of the departed. Drifting along the placid waters of the Acheron, shaded by towering trees and lush foliage, we're enveloped in a cloak of tranquility. Arriving at Necromanteion, we disembark to wander among ruins of temples and chambers, once the site of sacred rituals and divinations. Venturing into underground passageways, we marvel at the ingenuity of ancient engineers and the enduring power of myth and legend. Emerging into daylight, we're filled with a sense of wonder at the mysteries of the ancient world and grateful for the opportunity to unlock its secrets.

As our day trips from Corfu draw to a close, I hope you're inspired to embark on your own adventures and explore the rich history and natural beauty of the Ionian region. Whether cruising to nearby islands, delving into ancient ruins, or venturing into the heart of the Greek mainland, each excursion promises new discoveries and cherished memories. So, pack your bags, lace up your shoes, and get ready to embark on a journey of exploration and discovery in the enchanting lands beyond Corfu's shores.

CHAPTER 11

ITINERARIES AND SAMPLE PLANS

Join me on a journey of exploration as we delve into a variety of plans and itineraries to maximize your time in Corfu. Whether you're after a quick weekend escape, an immersion into culture, an outdoor adventure, a family-friendly outing, or a budget-friendly trip, I've got you covered with detailed recommendations and insider insights.

Weekend Getaway

Day 1: Arrival and Old Town Discovery

Arrive in Corfu and settle into your accommodation.

Begin your day by exploring the UNESCO World Heritage Site of Corfu Old Town, brimming with narrow streets, historic edifices, and cozy cafes.

Ascend the Old Fortress for sweeping vistas of the town and its harbor.

Treat yourself to a relaxed lunch at a traditional taverna, relishing local delights like moussaka and souvlaki.

Spend the afternoon meandering through the town's labyrinthine alleys, hunting for souvenirs, and soaking in the vibrant ambiance.

Come evening, dine at a waterfront eatery, marveling at the sunset over the Ionian Sea.

Day 2: Island Adventure and Beach Bliss

Kick off your day with a scrumptious Greek breakfast at a nearby cafe.

Opt for a car rental or join a guided tour to traverse Corfu's picturesque countryside and quaint villages.

Explore key attractions such as Achilleion Palace, Paleokastritsa Monastery, and the charming village of Pelekas.

Pause for a delightful lunch at a rustic taverna nestled in a quaint village.

Unwind in the afternoon on one of Corfu's stunning beaches like Glyfada or Agios Gordios.

Cap off the day with a leisurely seaside dinner, relishing fresh seafood and local wines.

Day 3: Nature Trek and Farewell

Begin your day with a nature hike in one of Corfu's scenic reserves like Mount Pantokrator or Korission Lagoon.

Enjoy a picnic amidst nature's splendor.

Spend the afternoon exploring Corfu's inland villages such as Kato Garouna or Lakones.

Return to Corfu Town for a final stroll through Old Town and bid adieu over dinner at a traditional taverna.

Depart from Corfu with cherished memories of a fulfilling weekend getaway teeming with culture, history, and natural allure.

Cultural Immersion

Day 1: Arrival and Historical Sojourn

Touch down in Corfu and settle into your lodgings.

Begin your day by traversing the historic lanes of Corfu Old Town, marveling at Venetian architecture, Byzantine churches, and quaint cafes.

Delve into the island's heritage at the Archaeological Museum of Corfu.

Relish a traditional Greek lunch at a local taverna, sampling delicacies like stifado and pastitsada.

In the afternoon, visit the Museum of Asian Art and the Museum of Solomos and Eminent Corfiots to delve deeper into the island's cultural connections.

In the evening, partake in a performance of traditional Greek music and dance at a local venue.

Day 2: Historical Exploration and Culinary Delights

Commence your day with a visit to Mon Repos Palace, birthplace of Prince Philip and a splendid example of neoclassical architecture.

Explore the nearby ruins of ancient Corfu, including the Temple of Artemis and the Monastery of Panagia Platytera.

Engage in a guided tour of Corfu's Venetian fortresses, learning about their strategic significance and architectural marvels.

Participate in a cooking class during the afternoon to master traditional Greek dishes like moussaka, tzatziki, and baklava.

Cap off the day with dinner at a local restaurant specializing in Corfiot cuisine, relishing dishes crafted with locally sourced ingredients.

Day 3: Nature and Cultural Exploration

Spend the morning discovering Corfu's charming inland villages like Pelekas, Doukades, and Sokraki, indulging in local flavors.

Visit the Byzantine Church of Agios Spyridon in Paleokastritsa village, home to Corfu's patron saint's relics.

Embark on a scenic coastal drive, pausing at scenic spots and beaches along the route.

In the afternoon, delve into the island's olive oil heritage at the Corfu Olive Oil Museum.

Conclude your evening with a leisurely dinner at a traditional taverna in Corfu Old Town, soaking in the ambiance.

Let's dive into a range of itineraries to make the most of your time in Corfu, from outdoor adventures to family-friendly trips and budget travel experiences.

Outdoor Adventure

Day 1: Island Arrival and Exploration

Arrive in Corfu and settle into your lodging.

Begin your day by exploring Corfu's rugged southern coast, where secluded beaches await for snorkeling, swimming, and sunbathing.

Enjoy a beach picnic with local treats like cheese, olives, and bread.

Afternoon kayaking or paddleboarding offers a chance to uncover hidden caves and rock formations.

Wrap up the day with a relaxing dinner at your accommodation.

Day 2: Hiking and Nature Discovery

Kick off your day with a hike up Mount Pantokrator for stunning island views.

Relish a picnic lunch surrounded by nature's splendor.

Explore the Korission Lagoon Nature Reserve, home to diverse bird species.

Join a guided nature walk to learn about Corfu's wetland ecosystem.

Conclude with a barbecue dinner under the stars.

Day 3: Watersports and Sunset Cruise

Dive into guided snorkeling or scuba diving to discover underwater wonders.

Savor a seafood lunch at a beachfront eatery.

Try windsurfing, kiteboarding, or parasailing in the afternoon.

Cap off with a sunset cruise along Corfu's coast.

Wrap up your adventure with a farewell dinner.

Family-Friendly Trip

Day 1: Beach Relaxation

Check into your family-friendly accommodation upon arrival.

Spend the morning at a kid-friendly beach like Agios Gordios.

Have a picnic lunch and explore nearby attractions.

Return for a family dinner at your lodging.

Day 2: Waterpark and Adventure Park

Hit Aqualand Corfu for waterslides and pools.

Enjoy a family-friendly lunch at the waterpark.

Head to Adventure Park Corfu for ziplining and rope courses.

Conclude with a family dinner and downtime.

Day 3: Animal Encounters and Nature Walks

Visit Corfu Donkey Rescue and enjoy lunch nearby.

Explore Corfu Butterfly Garden in the afternoon.

Cap off with a family dinner.

Budget Travel

Day 1: Old Town Exploration

Settle into budget-friendly accommodation.

Discover Corfu Old Town landmarks and enjoy local eats.

Explore museums offering discounted or free admission.

Return for a simple dinner.

Day 2: Island Discovery and Beach Day

Rent a bike or scooter for island exploration.

Relax at Glyfada Beach or Pelekas Beach with a picnic.

Opt for low-cost activities like hiking or snorkeling.

Conclude with a budget-friendly dinner.

Day 3: Nature and Cultural Exploration

Hike in Corfu's reserves and enjoy a picnic.

Visit free or low-cost attractions.

Stroll Corfu Old Town's streets.

End with a simple dinner.

No matter your style or budget, Corfu offers an itinerary to match. So gear up and get ready for a journey of discovery on this enchanting Greek island paradise.

CHAPTER 12

SAFETY TIPS AND GUIDELINES IN CORFU

Corfu, an idyllic island adorned with lively scenery, exquisite beaches, and a profound cultural legacy, captivates visitors with its charm. After immersing myself in its wonders, I've grasped the intricacies of ensuring safety while relishing all this paradise offers. This section is dedicated to guaranteeing not only a memorable but also a secure journey through Corfu. Let's delve into crucial safety advice and directives to navigate your Corfiot escapade seamlessly.

Sun Protection and Hydration

Sun Protection:

Corfu's sun shines intensely, particularly in the peak summer months from June to August. The Mediterranean climate ushers in potent UV levels, posing risks of sunburn and heat-related issues.

1. Apply Sunscreen: Always slather on high-SPF sunscreen (SPF 30 or above) at least 30 minutes before venturing outdoors. Reapply every two hours, or more frequently if swimming or perspiring.

2. Wear Protective Attire: Opt for lightweight, long-sleeved tops, broad-brimmed hats, and sunglasses to shield against the sun's rays. Consider UV-protective clothing for heightened sensitivity.

3. Seek Shade: Between 11 AM and 3 PM, the sun reaches its zenith. Seek sheltered spots during this period. Many beaches offer umbrellas for rent, while natural shade from trees abounds in parks and rural areas.

Hydration:

Staying hydrated is paramount, particularly under the Mediterranean sun.

1. Hydrate Adequately: Aim for a daily intake of at least 2 liters of water. Carry a reusable water bottle and utilize the numerous water fountains scattered across Corfu Town and other frequented areas.

2. Moderate Alcohol Consumption: While local wine and ouzo may tempt, remember that alcohol can lead to dehydration. If imbibing, ensure a balance with ample water intake.

3. Embrace Hydrating Foods: Infuse your diet with fruits and vegetables boasting high water content. Watermelon, cucumbers, oranges, and tomatoes not only refresh but also replenish hydration levels.

Water Safety and Beach Precautions

Corfu's stunning coastline beckons, yet vigilance is essential for a safe and enjoyable seaside experience.

Swimming Safety:

1. Stay within Designated Areas: Lifeguard-monitored swimming zones dot many of Corfu's beaches. Adhere to these demarcated areas and heed lifeguards' guidance and alerts.

2. Mind Rip Currents: Beware of rip currents, which can emerge where waves break. Stay composed if caught, swimming parallel to the shore until exiting the current, then returning to land.

3. Caution Regarding Marine Life: While Corfu's waters generally pose minimal risks, jellyfish stings may occur sporadically. Heed posted warnings and avoid swimming where jellyfish are sighted.

Beach Safety Measures

1. Safeguard Your Possessions: Beaches can become congested, and although Corfu is generally safe, it's wise to keep a vigilant eye on your belongings. Consider using a waterproof pouch for valuables or leaving non-essential items at your lodging.

2. Protect Your Feet: Sand can become scorching hot, and some beaches feature pebbles or rocks. Wearing water shoes can shield your feet from burns and injuries.

3. Maintain Hydration and Protection: As previously mentioned, prioritizing sun protection and hydration is crucial. Bring an ample supply of water, sunscreen, and either an umbrella or beach tent for shade.

Safety Recommendations for Crime and Personal Security

Corfu is renowned for its safety, yet like any bustling tourist destination, exercising vigilance and adopting sensible precautions is paramount.

Personal Safety:

1. Stick to Well-Illuminated Areas: During nighttime excursions, remain within well-lit and populated zones,

especially if alone. While Corfu Town and major tourist hubs are generally secure, exercising caution is advisable.

2. Reliable Transportation: Opt for registered taxis or reputable ride-hailing services. If renting a vehicle, ensure the rental agency is trustworthy and familiarize yourself with local driving regulations.

3. Minimize Displays of Wealth: Keep valuable possessions discreet. Flashy jewelry and high-end electronics may attract unwelcome attention.

Crime Prevention

1. Beware of Scams: Though infrequent, tourist scams can transpire. Exercise caution regarding overly friendly strangers offering unsolicited assistance or deals that appear too good to be true.

2. Secure Your Accommodations: Verify that your lodging offers robust security measures. Utilize the hotel safe for valuables and consistently lock doors and windows.

3. Emergency Contacts: Familiarize yourself with local emergency contact information. In Corfu, dial 112 for general emergencies. Identify the nearest police station and hospital for added preparedness.

Emergency Services and Healthcare Facilities

Familiarizing yourself with local emergency services and medical establishments can instill confidence and readiness in the event of an emergency.

Emergency Services

1. For General Emergencies: Dial 112 to summon assistance for police, fire, or medical emergencies. This universal number is applicable across the EU for various emergencies.

2. Local Contacts: Maintaining contact details for your accommodation, tour operators, and local acquaintances is beneficial. They can offer prompt assistance or guidance in emergent situations.

Medical Facilities

1. Hospitals: Corfu boasts several medical facilities, including the General Hospital of Corfu. Equipped to handle diverse emergencies, it is situated at 49 Lefkimmis Street, Corfu 491 00.

2. Pharmacies: Pharmacies abound in Corfu, providing over-the-counter medications and basic medical advice. Greek pharmacists are well-trained and can offer assistance

with minor ailments or direct you to a physician if necessary.

3. Travel Insurance: Ensure possession of comprehensive travel insurance encompassing medical emergencies. This coverage grants access to private medical services if required and caters to expenses linked with medical emergencies.

Wildlife and Environmental Risks

While Corfu typically lacks dangerous wildlife, it's essential to remain cautious to safeguard your well-being in natural settings.

Wildlife:

1. Reptiles and Insects: Corfu hosts various snakes and insects, most of which are harmless. Nevertheless, refrain from touching or disturbing wildlife. Seek immediate medical attention if bitten or stung.

2. Marine Life: As mentioned, occasional jellyfish sightings can occur. Additionally, sea urchins are prevalent in rocky regions, necessitating the use of water shoes to avert painful encounters.

Environmental Risks:

1. Hiking Safety: Adhere to marked trails while hiking and refrain from solo exploration in unfamiliar terrain. The landscape can be rugged, increasing the risk of getting lost.

2. Fire Hazards: Dry summer months elevate the likelihood of wildfires. Adhere to fire safety protocols, abstain from lighting fires, and promptly report any signs of fire.

3. Weather Conditions: While Corfu generally experiences mild weather, sudden storms may arise, particularly in autumn. Regularly monitor weather forecasts and adapt your plans accordingly.

Guidance for Solo Travelers and Families

Whether journeying alone or with loved ones, specific precautions ensure a secure and enjoyable experience.

Solo Travelers:

1. Maintain Connectivity: Keep in touch with friends or family, sharing your itinerary and checking in regularly.

2. Participate in Group Activities: Consider group tours or activities to enhance safety and foster social interaction.

3. Trust Your Intuition: If a situation or individual feels unsettling, trust your instincts and remove yourself from the scenario.

Families

1. Child Safety: Ensure constant supervision of young children, particularly near water. Utilize life jackets for water-based activities.

2. Opt for Family-Friendly Options: Select accommodations and activities catering to families, often featuring amenities and programs tailored for children.

3. Health Preparedness: Carry a first-aid kit containing essentials like band-aids, antiseptic cream, and any necessary prescription medications for your family.

Conclusion

Corfu presents a captivating destination abundant with cultural heritage and natural splendor. Adhering to these safety measures and guidelines ensures not only an enjoyable but also a secure trip. Whether relishing the sun on pristine shores, exploring ancient ruins, or trekking through lush landscapes, these precautions will enrich your experience in this enchanting island paradise. Remember, a safe journey is a joyful journey, and with adequate preparation and awareness, your Corfiot escapade promises nothing short of enchantment.

CHAPTER 13

CULTURAL ETIQUETTE AND CUSTOMS IN CORFU

Welcome to Corfu's rich cultural mosaic, where ancient practices blend seamlessly with contemporary values, crafting a distinct fusion of traditions and manners. Through my immersion in local life, I've learned that embracing and honoring these cultural subtleties can enhance your journey and forge deeper connections with the island and its inhabitants. Let's explore the captivating realm of Corfiot customs and etiquette.

Attire Guidelines and Modesty Considerations

Respectful Dressing:

Despite Corfu's relaxed ambiance, appropriate attire is crucial, particularly when visiting sacred sites or rural areas.

1. Covering Up: To show reverence, shoulders and knees should remain covered when entering churches or monasteries. Consider carrying a light scarf or shawl for this purpose.

2. Beachwear Protocol: While beach attire is suitable for the shore, it's deemed inappropriate for town centers or eateries. Remember to change or cover up before venturing into town.

3. Evening Dress Code: Opt for smart-casual attire, especially during evenings spent dining out or attending cultural affairs. Dressing up pays homage to the occasion and local customs.

Greetings and Social Etiquette

Warm Reception:

Corfiots are celebrated for their hospitality and amiable nature. Familiarizing yourself with local customs regarding greetings and social interactions can facilitate seamless engagement.

1. Courteous Greetings: Initiating conversations with a friendly "kalimera" (good morning), "kalispera" (good evening), or "kalinihta" (good night) sets a positive tone.

2. Handshakes and Air Kisses: Handshakes are customary in formal settings, while cheek kisses (air kisses) are prevalent in more informal contexts, typically starting with the right cheek.

3. Expressing Appreciation: A simple "efharisto" (thank you) is a gracious acknowledgment of kindness or hospitality received.

Tipping Practices and Service Standards

Gratuity Culture:

Although not as prevalent as in some nations, tipping is valued in Corfu as a token of appreciation for exceptional service.

1. Dining Establishments: While not obligatory, rounding up the bill or leaving a modest tip (5-10%) for outstanding service is customary.

2. Tour Guides and Drivers: Tipping tour guides and drivers is discretionary, but a small gratuity is a thoughtful gesture for exceptional service.

3. Accommodation Personnel: While not expected, offering a modest tip to hotel staff, such as housekeepers or bellhops, for exceptional service is welcomed.

Adherence to Local Customs and Traditions

Cultural Sensibility:

Respecting local customs and traditions is fundamental in Corfu, where age-old practices are deeply woven into daily life.

1. Religious Customs: Demonstrate reverence and modesty when visiting churches or participating in religious festivities.

2. Traditional Festivities: Embrace the local heritage by joining in traditional celebrations and festivals, such as Easter or local saints' days.

3. Dining Etiquette: When dining with locals, follow their lead regarding dining customs, including the sequence of courses and toasting protocols.

Photography Guidelines in Corfu

Privacy Consideration:

Corfu boasts captivating scenery and quaint villages, making it a haven for photographers. Nonetheless, it's crucial to respect locals' privacy and cultural norms when capturing images.

1. Permission Protocol: Always seek consent before photographing individuals, particularly if they're the focal point.

2. Privacy Adherence: Refrain from snapping pictures of private residences or individuals without approval, and be mindful of areas like cultural or religious sites where photography might be restricted.

3. Mutual Sharing: Consider sharing your captured moments with those you've photographed as a gesture of goodwill and appreciation.

Language Assistance and Basic Greek Phrases

Embracing the Vernacular:

While English suffices in tourist hubs, acquainting yourself with a few fundamental Greek phrases can foster connections and demonstrate regard for local culture.

1. Essential Greetings: Familiarize yourself with basic salutations such as "yasou" (hello), "efharisto" (thank you), and "parakalo" (please).

2. Courteous Inquiries: Proficiency in polite inquiries like "signomi" (excuse me) or "sighnomi, milate anglika?"

(excuse me, do you speak English?) can prove immensely beneficial.

3. Pronunciation Practice: Pay heed to pronunciation as it can significantly enhance communication and endear you to locals.

In Conclusion

Grasping and honoring Corfu's cultural etiquette and traditions is pivotal for a gratifying and respectful travel experience. By adhering to modest attire, extending warm and respectful greetings to locals, and embracing local customs and traditions, you'll not only enrich your journey but also cultivate meaningful bonds with the island and its inhabitants. So, as you embark on your Corfu adventure, remember to tread thoughtfully, immerse yourself in the local ethos, and relish every moment in this culturally affluent and dynamic locale. Kaló taxídi (bon voyage)!

CHAPTER 14

DOS AND DON'TS IN CORFU

As you explore the captivating island of Corfu, it's vital to proceed with care and honor the local customs, traditions, and environment. Here are some guidelines to assist you in navigating Corfu with elegance, cultural sensitivity, and environmental awareness.

Respect for Local Traditions and Customs

Do's:

1. Embrace the Heritage: Immerse yourself in Corfu's vibrant tapestry of traditions and customs. Engage in local festivals, partake in religious observances, and absorb the island's history from its inhabitants.

2. Display Respect: When visiting religious sites or cultural gatherings, dress modestly and conduct yourself with reverence. Adhere to guidelines, covering your shoulders and knees upon entering churches or monasteries.

3. Connect with Locals: Initiate conversations with the welcoming locals and demonstrate genuine curiosity about their traditions and way of life. Learning some basic Greek phrases can facilitate meaningful connections.

Don'ts:

1. Disrespect Sacred Spaces: Refrain from inappropriate behavior or loud disturbances when visiting religious or historical locations. Avoid touching artifacts and maintain the sanctity of these revered sites.

2. Neglect Local Customs: Respect and adhere to local customs and traditions, even if they differ from your own. Exercise cultural sensitivity, refraining from public displays of affection in conservative settings.

3. Ignore Signage: Heed signage and comply with instructions at archaeological sites or cultural landmarks. Disregarding regulations not only disrespects these sites but also jeopardizes their preservation.

Environmental Conservation Practices

Do's:

1. Reduce, Reuse, Recycle: Practice responsible waste management by minimizing plastic usage, repurposing items, and adhering to local recycling protocols.

2. Support Sustainable Tourism: Opt for eco-conscious accommodations, dining establishments, and tour operators that prioritize environmental sustainability. Engage in activities that leave minimal impact on the natural surroundings.

3. Leave No Trace: Preserve Corfu's natural beauty by leaving no trace of your visit. Dispose of waste properly, refrain from disturbing wildlife or vegetation, and stick to designated paths to minimize environmental impact.

Don'ts:

1. Littering: Never discard litter, whether you're on the beach, in rural areas, or within city limits. Dispose of waste responsibly and utilize designated bins whenever available.

2. Harming Coral Reefs: When snorkeling or diving, avoid touching or stepping on coral reefs, as they are fragile ecosystems vulnerable to human interference.

3. Feeding Wildlife: Resist the urge to feed wild animals, as it disrupts their natural behaviors and may lead to dependency on human-provided food. Observe wildlife from a respectful distance without intervening.

Appropriate Conduct at Archaeological Sites

Guidelines:

1. Show Reverence for Heritage Sites: Handle archaeological sites with care and respect as they hold immense value in Corfu's history and cultural tapestry. Adhere to marked paths, refrain from scaling ruins, and avoid touching ancient relics.

2. Follow Guide Instructions: When accompanied by a guide at an archaeological site, attentively listen to their explanations and comply with any directives provided. Guides offer valuable insights into the site's significance and backstory.

3. Report Misconduct: If you witness any acts of vandalism or unauthorized excavation at archaeological sites, promptly inform the authorities. Safeguarding these sites is a collective responsibility.

Avoid:

1. Defacement or Removal: Never deface or tamper with archaeological sites by carving initials, adding graffiti, or pilfering artifacts. Such actions not only harm the site but also deprive future generations of their cultural legacy.

2. Artifact Disturbance: It's illegal and unethical to extract artifacts or souvenirs from archaeological sites. Preserve the site's integrity and historical value by leaving everything undisturbed.

3. Disregard Safety Signs: Take heed of safety signs and cautions at archaeological sites, especially regarding restricted areas or potential dangers. Ignoring these warnings jeopardizes your safety and that of the site.

Interaction with Wildlife and Marine Life

Best Practices:

1. Observe from a Distance: Maintain a safe distance from wildlife encounters to avoid disrupting their natural behavior. Utilize binoculars or a zoom lens for a closer view without intrusion.

2. Marine Life Protection: Practice responsible behavior when snorkeling or diving, refraining from touching or harming coral reefs and avoiding chasing or disturbing marine creatures.

3. Conservation Support: Familiarize yourself with local conservation initiatives and contribute to organizations dedicated to preserving Corfu's biodiversity and habitats.

Avoid:

1. Wildlife Feeding: Refrain from feeding wild animals to prevent disruption of their natural feeding habits and potential risks to both animals and humans.

2. Nesting Site Disturbance: Respect nesting sites of birds or sea turtles by maintaining distance and adhering to posted guidelines for their protection.

3. Ocean Pollution: Dispose of waste properly and refrain from littering, particularly near beaches or water bodies. Plastic pollution poses a significant threat to marine life, necessitating responsible waste management.

Safety Measures for Outdoor Activities

Recommendations:

1. Plan Ahead: Conduct thorough research, check weather forecasts, and outline your route before embarking on outdoor excursions. Inform someone of your plans and expected return time for safety.

2. Hydration: Carry an ample water supply and stay hydrated, especially in hot weather. Consistently hydrate, even if not feeling thirsty, to prevent dehydration.

3. Essential Gear: Pack essentials like sunscreen, insect repellent, a first aid kit, and navigation tools to be prepared for emergencies and unforeseen circumstances.

Avoid:

1. Overexertion: Know your physical limits and pace yourself during outdoor activities, particularly in extreme conditions, to prevent exhaustion or injury.

2. Neglecting Safety Equipment: Wear appropriate safety gear, such as helmets, life jackets, or hiking boots, for activities like hiking, biking, or watersports. Safety should always be prioritized over convenience.

3. Straying from Trails: Stick to designated trails and pathways to avoid damaging fragile ecosystems and minimize the risk of getting lost or encountering hazards.

Principles of Responsible Tourism

Recommendations:

1. Support Local Enterprises: Opt for locally-owned accommodations, eateries, and stores to bolster the local economy and foster sustainable tourism. Seek authentic experiences that contribute positively to the community.

2. Show Consideration to Locals: Respect local customs, traditions, and sensibilities, treating residents with kindness and deference. Engage authentically with locals and express gratitude for their hospitality and cultural heritage.

3. Make a Positive Contribution: Minimize your environmental footprint, honor wildlife and natural habitats, and engage in responsible tourism initiatives to leave a beneficial impact on the places you visit.

Avoid:

1. Engaging in Harmful Practices: Steer clear of activities that harm the environment, deplete local resources, or disrespect cultural norms. Be a conscientious traveler and leave Corfu in a better state than you found it.

2. Endorsing Unethical Ventures: Refuse to support businesses or activities involved in unethical practices like

wildlife exploitation, environmental harm, or cultural appropriation. Opt for responsible alternatives that uphold sustainability and ethical standards.

3. Ignoring Local Regulations: Familiarize yourself with local laws and regulations, ensuring compliance throughout your stay in Corfu. Lack of awareness is no excuse, so make a concerted effort to honor and adhere to local ordinances and directives.

By adhering to these guidelines, you can relish a fulfilling experience in Corfu while honoring the island's heritage, environment, and community. Remember, as a visitor, your actions wield influence in shaping a legacy of responsible tourism for generations to come.

Conclusion and Farewell

As my time exploring the captivating island of Corfu comes to an end, I find myself reminiscing about the countless experiences and unforgettable moments that have enriched my stay. From the sun-kissed beaches and ancient landmarks to the warm hospitality and diverse cultural heritage, Corfu has truly left an indelible mark on my heart, leaving me with cherished memories to treasure forever. As I bid farewell to this enchanting island, let me offer a summary of its key highlights, provide some final advice for visitors, and express a heartfelt goodbye.

Corfu's Key Highlights in Summary

Corfu boasts lush landscapes, crystal-clear waters, and a vibrant culture, offering a plethora of attractions and experiences for every traveler. Here are some of the island's standout features:

1. Natural Splendor: From the azure shores of Paleokastritsa to the verdant slopes of Mount Pantokrator, Corfu's natural beauty is simply breathtaking. Discover hidden coves, traverse scenic trails, and soak up the Mediterranean sun amid stunning scenery.

2. Historic Marvels: Transport yourself back in time as you explore Corfu's historical landmarks, including the magnificent Achilleion Palace, the imposing Old Fortress, and the charming streets of Corfu Old Town. Each site embodies the island's rich history and cultural legacy.

3. Cultural Immersion: Immerse yourself in Corfu's vibrant culture by partaking in traditional festivals, savoring local cuisine, and engaging with the welcoming locals. From lively tavernas to quaint villages, the island exudes hospitality and camaraderie.

4. Outdoor Adventures: Whether you're an adrenaline junkie or a nature enthusiast, Corfu offers a myriad of outdoor activities to suit every preference. From hiking and water sports to boat excursions and horseback riding, there's no shortage of adventures amidst the island's stunning landscapes.

5. Gastronomic Delights: Treat your taste buds to Corfu's exquisite cuisine, which melds traditional Greek flavors with Mediterranean influences. From fresh seafood and

local delicacies to olive oil tastings and wine tours, the island is a paradise for food enthusiasts.

Final Advice for Visitors

Before embarking on your Corfu escapade, here are some parting tips to ensure a memorable and enjoyable journey:

1. Cultural Respect: Be mindful of local customs and traditions, and show reverence for the island's cultural heritage. Dress modestly when visiting religious sites, greet locals warmly, and embrace the relaxed island pace.

2. Environmental Conservation: Practice responsible tourism by minimizing your environmental impact, supporting eco-conscious businesses, and leaving no trace behind. Respect wildlife and natural habitats, and stick to designated trails when exploring nature.

3. Safety First: Prioritize your safety by staying hydrated, applying sunscreen, and taking necessary precautions during outdoor activities. Familiarize yourself with local laws and regulations, and trust your instincts when navigating unfamiliar terrain.

4. Embrace the Experience: Let go of expectations and fully immerse yourself in the sights, sounds, and flavors of Corfu. Embrace spontaneity, be open to new experiences, and cherish every moment of your adventure.

A Fond Farewell from the Author

As I bid adieu to Corfu, I carry with me a treasure trove of memories and a deep appreciation for the island's beauty and warmth. From its turquoise coastlines to its rugged mountains, Corfu has left an indelible impression on my soul, reminding me of the transformative power of travel and the boundless wonders of our world. To all those who have shared in this journey, I extend my heartfelt gratitude and warmest wishes. May your own adventures in Corfu be filled with joy, discovery, and the magic of this enchanting island.

Corfu Glossary

Before we part ways, here's a glossary of Corfu terms to help you navigate the local language and culture:

1. Kalimera: Good morning

2. Kalispera: Good evening

3. Kalinihta: Good night

4. Yasou: Hello/Goodbye

5. Efharisto: Thank you

6. Parakalo: Please/You're welcome

7. Taverna: Traditional Greek restaurant

8. Meze: Small dishes served as appetizers

9. Ouzo: Anise-flavored alcoholic drink

10. Kefi: Joy, zest for life

With these memories and words, I bid you farewell and wish you safe travels on your own journey through the timeless beauty of Corfu. Until we meet again, may your adventures be filled with wonder, discovery, and the enduring spirit of exploration.

Kaló taxídi! (Bon voyage!)

CHAPTER 15

APPENDIX: USEFUL RESOURCES

As your time in Corfu concludes, having access to essential resources can greatly enhance your experience and provide necessary support. This appendix includes a list of valuable resources, such as emergency contacts, maps, additional reading materials, and useful local phrases to help you navigate the island effortlessly.

Emergency Contacts

Police:

For emergencies or legal assistance, contact the local police department. For more information, visit: Hellenic Police (http://www.police.gov.gr).

Ambulance:

In medical emergencies or when urgent medical assistance is required, dial the ambulance service. More details can be found at: Emergency Rescue Service (http://www.emergencyrescue.gr).

Fire Department:

If you encounter a fire or need help with fire-related incidents, contact the fire department immediately. Visit: Fire Service (http://www.fire.gr) for more information.

Tourist Police:

Tourists needing assistance with lost belongings or travel-related issues can contact the tourist police. More details are available at: Tourist Police (http://www.touristpolice.gr).

Coast Guard:

For assistance at sea or during water activities, contact the coast guard. Visit: Hellenic Coast Guard (http://www.hcg.gr) for more information.

Maps and Navigational Tools

Google Maps:

An indispensable tool for navigating Corfu's streets, beaches, and landmarks. Use [Google Maps](http://www.google.com/maps) to plan routes, find nearby attractions, and get real-time directions.

Corfu Tourist Map:

A detailed map showcasing Corfu's main attractions, beaches, and points of interest. Available at tourist information centers, hotels, and online at: Corfu Tourist Map (http://www.corfutouristmap.com).

OpenStreetMap:

An open-source mapping platform offering detailed maps of Corfu, including hiking trails, cycling routes, and rural roads. Check: OpenStreetMap (http://www.openstreetmap.org) for comprehensive maps.

Corfu Bus Routes:

For public transportation, consult: Corfu Bus Routes (http://www.corfubusroutes.com) to find schedules, routes, and fare information.

Additional Reading and References

Visit Greece:

The official tourism website of Greece, providing information on Corfu's attractions, events, and travel tips. It also includes practical details on transportation, accommodations, and dining options. Check: Visit Greece (http://www.visitgreece.gr)

Corfu History:

For a deeper exploration of Corfu's history and culture, this website offers articles, photos, and resources on the island's rich heritage. Visit: Corfu History (http://www.corfuhistory.eu) for more information.

Useful Local Phrases

- Yasou (Γειά σου): Hello/Goodbye

- Parakalo (Παρακαλώ): Please/You're welcome

- Efharisto (Ευχαριστώ): Thank you

- Kalimera (Καλημέρα): Good morning

- Kalinihta (Καληνύχτα): Good night

- Ti kaneis? (Τι κάνεις): How are you?

- Kali orexi (Καλή όρεξη): Enjoy your meal

- Kefi (Κέφι): Joy, zest for life

Website Links

1. www.fire.gr

2. www.hcg.gr

3. www.google.com/maps

4. www.visitgreece.gr

5. www.openstreetmap.org

6. www.corfuhistory.eu

With these resources, you will be well-prepared to navigate Corfu confidently and make the most of your time on this enchanting island. Whether you are exploring ancient ruins, relaxing on sun-drenched beaches, or indulging in traditional Greek cuisine, may your journey be filled with wonder, discovery, and unforgettable experiences. Safe travels, and until we meet again in the timeless beauty of Corfu!

Addresses and Locations of Popular Accommodation

Luxury Resorts

1. Kontokali Bay Resort & Spa

   Address: Kontokali, 49100, Corfu

   Website: www.kontokalibay.com)

2. MarBella Corfu Hotel

   Address: Agios Ioannis Peristeron, 49084, Corfu

3. Corfu Imperial, Grecotel Exclusive Resort

   Address: Kommeno, 49083, Corfu

Website: www.grecotel.com/i

4. Ikos Dassia

Address: Dassia Bay, 49100, Corfu

Website: www.ikosresorts.com/resorts/ikos-dassia

5. Angsana Corfu Resort & Spa

Address: Benitses, 49084, Corfu

Website: www.angsana.com/en/greece/corfu

Budget-Friendly Hotels

1. Sunshine Hotel & Apartments

Address: Sidari, 49081, Corfu

2. Dalia Hotel

Address: Garitsa Bay, 49100, Corfu

3. Ariti Grand Hotel

Address: Nafsikas 41, Kanoni, 49100, Corfu

4. Atlantis Hotel

Address: Xenofontos Stratigou 48, 49100, Corfu

Website: www.atlantis-hotel-corfu.com)

5. Elli Marina Studios & Apartments

Address: Benitses, 49084, Corfu

Website: www.ellimarina.com

Boutique Guesthouses

1. Bella Venezia Hotel

Address: 4 Zambeli, 49100, Corfu

2. Siora Vittoria Boutique Hotel

Address: Stefanou Padova 36, 49100, Corfu

Website: www.sioravittoria.com

3. Arcadion Hotel

Address: 2 Vlasopoulou & Kapodistriou, 49100, Corfu

Website: www.arcadionhotel.com

4. Secret Garden Apartments

Address: Gouvia, 49100, Corfu

5. The Merchant's House

Address: Old Perithia, 49081, Corfu

Website: www.themerchantshousecorfu.com

Unique Stays

1. Pelekas Monastery Hotel

Address: Pelekas Beach, 49084, Corfu

Website: www.pelekasmonastery.com

2. Corfu Luxury Villas

Address: Prinias, 49100, Corfu

Website: www.corfuvillas.com

3. Art Hotel Debono

Address: Gouvia, 49100, Corfu

4. Roda Beach Resort & Spa

Address: Roda, 49081, Corfu

Website: www.mitsishotels.com

5. Casa Lucia

Address: Sgombou, 49100, Corfu

Addresses and Locations of Popular Restaurants and Cafés

Restaurants

1. Avli Restaurant

Address: 8 Panou Aravantinou, 49100, Corfu

Website: www.avlicorfu.com)

2. Venetian Well

Address: Kalocheretou 22, 49100, Corfu

3. Rex Restaurant

Address: Kapodistriou 66, 49100, Corfu

4. The White House Restaurant

Address: Kalami, 49083, Corfu

Website: www.thewhitehouse.gr)

5. Taverna Agni

   Address: Agni Bay, 49100, Corfu

   Website: www.tavernaagni.com)

Cafes

1. Pomo D'Oro Wine Restaurant
   Address: 28th Oktovriou 15, 49100, Corfu

2. Mikro Café
   Address: Mavili Square, 49100, Corfu

3. Liston Café
   Address: Kapodistriou, 49100, Corfu

4. Cafe Yali
   Address: Faliraki, 49100, Corfu

5. Rosmarino
   Address: Agias Sofias 2, 49100, Corfu

   Website: www.rosmarino.com)

Addresses and Locations of Popular Bars and Clubs

Bars

1. Bristol Cafe Bar

   Address: 1, Nikiforou Theotoki, 49100, Corfu

2. The Old Barrel

   Address: Benitses, 49084, Corfu

3. Why Cocktail Industry

   Address: Kapodistriou 96, 49100, Corfu

4. Barbarossa Bar

   Address: Kommeno, 49100, Corfu

5. Cafe Bristol

   Address: 1 Filarmonikis, 49100, Corfu

Clubs

1. 54 Dreamy Nights

Address: Eth. Antistaseos 54, 49100, Corfu

Website: www.54dreamynights.com)

2. Montecristo Club

Address: Eth. Lefkimis 40, 49084, Corfu

3. Aqua Nightclub

Address: Kavos, 49080, Corfu

4. Edem Beach Club

Address: Dassia, 49100, Corfu

5. Sway Club Corfu

Address: Ipsos, 49100, Corfu

Addresses and Locations of Top Attractions

1. Achilleion Palace

Address: Gastouri, 49084, Corfu

Website: www.achillion-corfu.gr)

2. Old Fortress of Corfu

Address: Palaia Anaktora, 49100, Corfu

3. Liston Promenade

Address: Spianada Square, 49100, Corfu

Website: www.visitcorfu.com

4. Paleokastritsa Monastery

Address: Paleokastritsa, 49083, Corfu

5. Sidari Beach and Canal d'Amour

Address: Sidari, 49081, Corfu

6. Mount Pantokrator

Address: Strinilas, 49083, Corfu

7. Corfu Old Town

Address: Corfu Town, 49100, Corfu

These carefully selected addresses and locations will guide you to some of the finest accommodations, dining venues, nightlife, and attractions in Corfu.

Whether you seek luxury or budget-friendly options, a serene café or a vibrant club, or are keen on exploring historical landmarks and natural beauty, Corfu offers something for every traveler.

Enjoy your trip and make the most of your time on this captivating island!

Truthfinders

6825 Paiute tN
Niwot
CO 80503

Phone 805 570-4624

Johnhermancfp@verizon.com

Aug pg 1995 (DOB

Daniel L Herman Heather
John C Herman H Heln
Lyla cherry Herman
Harmony Miller
Thomas H Herman
Associate
Roger
Crocker